LITTLE RABBITS

BROWN RABBIT'S
SHAPES

ALAN BAKER

KINGFISHER
NEW YORK

KINGFISHER
LONDON & NEW YORK

First published 1994 by Kingfisher
This edition published 2017 by Kingfisher
Published in the United States by Kingfisher,
175 Fifth Ave., New York, NY 10010
Kingfisher is an imprint of Macmillan Children's Books, London.
All rights reserved.

Copyright © Alan Baker 1994

Distributed in the U.S. and Canada by Macmillan,
175 Fifth Ave., New York, NY 10010

Library of Congress Cataloging-in-Publication data
has been applied for.

ISBN: 978-0-7534-7326-9 (HB)
ISBN: 978-0-7534-7327-6 (PB)

Kingfisher books are available for special promotions
and premiums. For details contact: Special Markets
Department, Macmillan, 175 Fifth Ave.,
New York, NY 10010.

For more information, please visit
www.kingfisherbooks.com

Printed in China
9 8 7 6 5 4 3 2 1
1TR/1116/WKT/UG/157MA

One day a package arrived
for Brown Rabbit.
It had bright red triangles
on the wrapping paper.

The card was
the shape of a
rectangle. It said
"To Brown Rabbit."

Rabbit took off the paper. Underneath was a square box. Rabbit lifted the lid.

Inside was
a tube ...

... with a circle shape top.
Rabbit opened it.

Out tumbled
five flat floppy
balloons,
all different
colors.

Lovely balloons,
just waiting
to be blown up.

Rabbit blew up the red balloon.
It was big and round like a ball.

Whoosh! It flew off.

The orange balloon was
oval-shaped like an egg.

Whoosh! Away it flew.

The green balloon was l o n g
and sausage-shaped.
Rabbit couldn't hold it.
Whoo-whoosh!
Off it went.

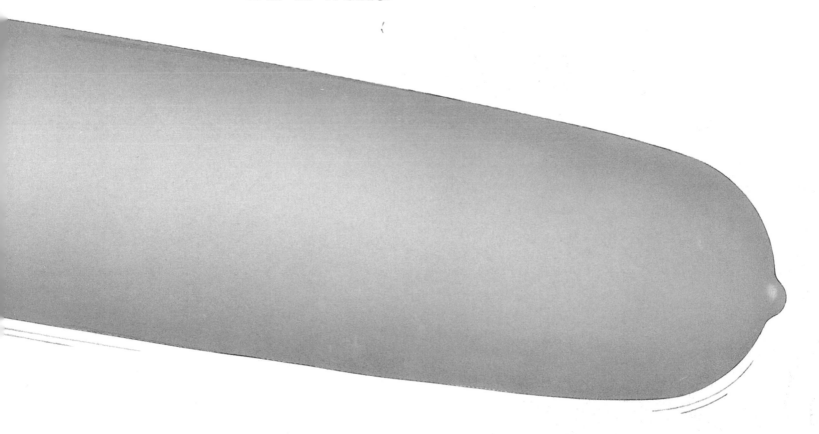

The purple balloon
was smaller and
shaped like a pear.

One more puff, thought Rabbit.
Then BANG! It burst.

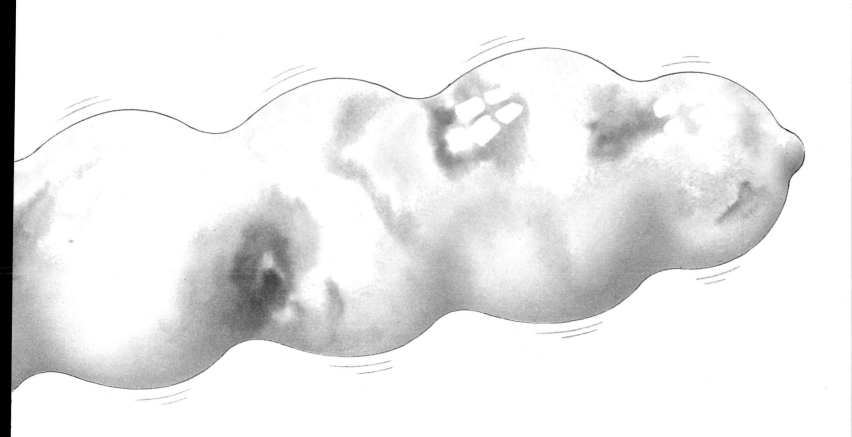

The last balloon was all colors,
l o n g and curly-wurly.

Whoosh! Blast off!

Whoo ... Whoo ... Whoo-oosh!

Goodbye, balloon shapes.
I'm all out of puff,
thought Rabbit.

He tidied up the balloons,
the tube, the box,
and the paper.

Then rabbit-shaped Rabbit
fell fast asleep on top.